Thank you to the generous team who gave their time and talents to make this book possible:

Authors
Second grade students at
Monarch Academy Public Charter
School in Glen Burnie, MD

Illustrators
Second grade students at
Monarch Academy Public Charter
School in Glen Burnie, MD

Creative Directors
Caroline Kurtz, Jane Kurtz,
and Kenny Rasmussen

Translator
Somali Region State Education Bureau

Designer
Beth Crow

Ready Set Go Books, an Open Hearts Big Dreams Project

Special thanks to Ethiopia Reads donors and staff for believing in this project and helping get it started-- and for arranging printing, distribution, and training in Ethiopia.

ISBN: 979-8726831374
Library of Congress Control Number: 2021906014

Publication Date: 3/23/21

The Busy Little Bee

Shinidii yarayd ee mashquulsanayd

English and Somali

A busy little bee is
buzz, buzz, buzzing
in the forest.

Shinidii yarayd ee
mashquulka ahayd way
guuxaysaa, guuxaysaa,
waxy guuxaysaa kaynta
dhexdeeda.

The busy little bee
sees pretty plants
and large green
trees in the forest.

Shinidii yarayd ee mashquulsanayd waxy kaynta ku aragtay dhir qurux badan iyo geedo waawayn oo cagaar ah.

The busy little bee
needs nectar from
plants to make honey.

Shinada yari waxay ubaahantahay dheecaanka midhaha si ay usamayso malab.

It's time for pollination!

Waa wakhtigay rimayeen

The busy little bee lands on a coffee flower to take sweet nectar.

Shinidii yarayd waxay ku dul dagtay ubixii bunka si ay uga qaadato neecaanka macaan.

The busy little bee
also gets pollen on
its hairy body.

Shinidii yarayd waxay
sidoo kale mankii ku
qaadatay timihii jidhkeeda
kuyaalay.

The busy little bee flies to a new coffee flower.

Shinidii yarayd waxay
uduushay ubaxa bun cusub.

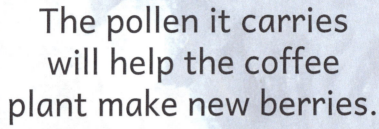

The pollen it carries
will help the coffee
plant make new berries.

Shinidii yarayd waxay
uduushay ubaxa bun cusub.

Those new berries will
make farmers happy.

Midhahan cusub waxy
farxad galin doonaan
beeralayda.

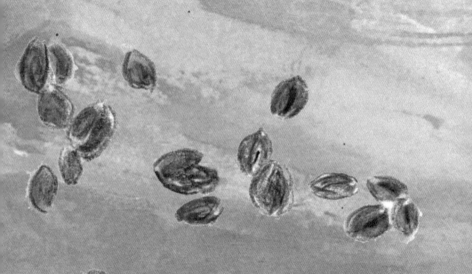

Those new berries will also make people who drink coffee happy.

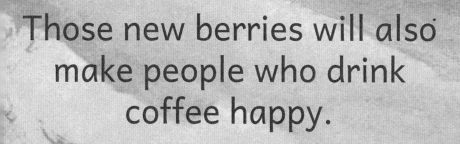

Midhaha cusubi waxay
sidoo kale farxad galin
doonaan dadka bunka caba.

Bees help trees and
trees help bees!

Shinidu waxay caawisaa
geedaha, geeduhuna
waxay caawiyaan shinida.

All the busy bees help
everyone who loves coffee.

Dhamaan shinidu waxay
caawisaa qof kasta kaas oo
jecel bunka.

About The Authors and Illustrators

Second grade students at Monarch Academy Public Charter School in Glen Burnie, MD researched pollinators and used their knowledge to write and illustrate this book in the spring of 2019. In their classrooms, students learned about the life cycle of plants, the importance of pollinators, threats to pollinators, and how to become activists for pollinators. In art class, students looked closely at photos of bees, coffee plants, and Ethiopian landscapes to create their collage illustrations. Students hope that this book helps spread awareness of the importance of bees and other pollinators!

Monarch Academy Public Charter School is an affiliate of the TranZed Alliance and partners with EL Education to provide a curriculum that fosters growth and achievement for all students through authentic learning experiences. Through a Fund for Teachers grant, the team of teachers guiding our authors and illustrators through their work were able to visit Ethiopia to gain first hand experience to further student learning.

About Ready Set Go Books

Reading has the power to change lives, but many children and adults in Ethiopia cannot read. One reason is that Ethiopia doesn't have enough books in local languages to give people a chance to practice reading. Ready Set Go books wants to close that gap and open a world of ideas and possibilities for kids and their communities.

When you buy a Ready Set Go book, you provide critical funding to create and distribute more books.

Learn more at:
http://openheartsbigdreams.org/book-project/

About Ethiopia Reads

 Ethiopia Reads was started by volunteers in places like Grand Forks, North Dakota; Denver, Colorado; San Francisco, California; and Washington D.C. who wanted to give the gift of reading to more kids in Ethiopia. One of the founders, Jane Kurtz, learned to read in Ethiopia where she spent most of her childhood and where the circle of life has come around to bring her Ethiopian-American grandchildren. As a children's book author, Jane is the driving force behind Open Hearts Big Dreams Ready Set Go Books - working to create the books that inspire those just learning to read.

About Open Hearts Big Dreams

 Open Hearts Big Dreams began as a volunteer organization, led by Ellenore Angelidis in Seattle, Washington, to provide sustainable funding and strategic support to Ethiopia Reads, collaborating with Jane Kurtz. OHBD has now grown to be its own nonprofit organization supporting literacy, innovation, and leadership for young people in Ethiopia.

Ellenore Angelidis comes from a family of teachers who believe education is a human right, and opportunity should not depend on your birthplace. And as the adoptive mother of a little girl who was born in Ethiopia and learned to read in the U.S., as well as an aspiring author, she finds the chance to positively impact literacy hugely compelling!

About the Language

Somali is an Afroasiatic language belonging to the Cushitic branch. Somali is spoken in Somalia, Somaliland, Djibouti, Ethiopia and Kenya. It is used as an adoptive language by a few neighboring ethnic groups and individuals. Somali was not written until the Osmanya alphabet was developed in 1920. The Latin alphabet was adopted in 1972.

About the Translation

The Somali Regional State, also known as Soomaali Galbeed, is the second largest and easternmost of the regions of Ethiopia. The regional state borders the Ethiopian states of Afar and Oromia and the city of Dire Dawa to the west, as well as Djibouti and Somaliland to the north and northeast, Somalia to the east and south; and Kenya to the southwest. Somali Region State Education Bureau worked with Ethiopia Reads to translate this title as part of a local printing project for regional schools and libraries.

Over 100 unique Ready Set Go books available!

 To view all available titles on Amazon, search "Ready Set Go Ethiopia" or scan QR code

 Chaos

 Not Ready!

 We Can Stop the Lion

 Talk Talk Turtle

 The Glory of Gondar

 Giraffe and Me

 Fifty Lemons

 Big, Bigger, Biggest

Open Heart Big Dreams is pleased to offer discounts for bulk orders, educators and organizations.

Contact ellenore@openheartsbigdreams.org for more information.

Made in the USA
Monee, IL
18 June 2021